STRETCH MARKS IN WATER

Odule O'Sussane

Poems & Prose Poems

To my Mother [& late Grandmother].

To the ever-painful process of sorting through what is trauma and what is your engrained personality. To the people lost this year. To putting back your life together amidst loss. To my late friend. To tender loving friendship that did not hold itself back.

ODULE . O'SUSSANE
STRETCH MARKS IN WATER

"When does a war end? When can I say your name and have it mean only your name and not what you left behind?"

Ocean Vuong

Ma, we do not exist together anymore, but the cycle of us runs on loop in these poems.

---

[1] STRETCH MARKS IN WATER

CONTENTS

I'm A Collection Of The Women Who Made Me

I.

1. Photographs Of Hands

2. Where I'm From

3. I Stand Still

4. Same Old

5. A Poem Written Into A Voice Memo On The Toll Road

II.

1. The Past Beats Inside Me Like A Second Heart

2. My Body Is A Sickness Called Anger (i)

3. My Body Is A Sickness Called Anger (ii)

4. Untangling Anger

III.

1. Mamia

2. Cathedral

3. The Strawberry Patch

4. Mothers

5. Bones

IV.

1. The Depression Gets Real With Me

2. Bracelets

3. Emotional Abuse Works Like This

4. Pattern Of Abuse

5. This Is How It Goes No Matter Which City I'm In

V.

1. My Friend Once Threw Up On My Front Porch

2. Heat Wave

3. Daniella George - My Friend From Down Under

4. Bless The Crazy Femmes

5. Bless The Healing

• Notes

• Acknowledgments

---

[2] STRETCH MARKS IN WATER

I'm A Collection Of The Women Who Made Me.

My gran-gran gave her daughter a spirit

so fierce that the sky couldn't hold it.

My grandmother gave her daughter the

strength to carry the universe inside her.

I open my mouth and hear the voice of

my mother who echoes the words of my

grandmother, who learned the word 'no'

before she learned her own name.

Sometimes, when I look in the mirror,

I'm not sure whose face I see.

I owe everything I am to the women

who came before me.

STRETCH MARKS IN WATER

Photographs Of Hands.

My Mother's

I've never noticed the way her fingers caress her bottle, a gesture as familiar as holding a child. Her hands are witnesses: kneading dough, baking pies, lifting herself over balcony railings, an expression of joy I've never seen pass across her face lives in a photograph. Her hands know she's pregnant before she does. They swell with new life when she holds me, my small hands sinking into hers - palms marked with lines connected to another life. Her thumbs and index fingers callused, thick skin protecting her from old wounds unhealed, left underneath until split open, revealing years of things abandoned. Hands held her in place while she negotiated her brother's release from custody - the man tells her to retrieve her brother's shoes so he doesn't hang himself with shoelaces.

Hands are her tool for survival; she whisks flour, turns water into soup, all on a hotplate on the floor.

My Father's

It took me a long time to realize my father had hands. When I was young, I would watch him sign my school agenda. He would take my small hand in his and we would trace over the letters of his name together, a final flick of a *T* whispered memories; starving hands shaping and joining metals in a smithy. Twenty years later, I come home late and find him sitting on the couch, hunched over the dining table with a blackened sausage in one hand and half a loaf in the other. He ate late at night what he forgot to eat during the day.

Hands now freely hold food with reminders of starvation remaining in his callused palms. His hands flatten dough, clean apartments, become tools instead of body parts. The edges of his fingernails yellowed by metal rust paints. His hands smell of history, soil and sweat from morning runs around the farm.

STRETCH MARKS IN WATER

Where I'm From.

I am from loud voices, ones that

never hear you ask for a cup of

water, a breath of fresh air, or

a hand to hold.

I am from wrinkly grandpas without

grandmas because they are far above,

meeting God with a warm sunshine

smile - finally forgiven.

From cigarette smoke and the phrase;

I'll stop when I'm skinny.

No, I don't believe you,

I know we're all addicted to something.

We have to remind ourselves of

how easily we perish.

From big scoops of ice cream while

my dad tells me that his mother

used to be beautiful.

From women who only talk about grocery store prices because they have spent their whole lives at the checkout counter, waiting for a man to tell them they were worth more than celery sticks and strawberry wine.

From boyfriends and girlfriends, cousins that take their date to the shed and kiss strawberry wine soaked lips and whisper,
i need you, please do not leave me.
like a family heirloom.
We've always confused the words need and love, they roll off tongues like sinister synonyms.

From boys that look at my younger cousin, my baby girl and call her baby.

They make her forget the time she was brave, they kiss her so hard that she forgets that I believe in her, that God believes in her.

I'm from mistakes that no one forgets.
From the miserable grey of the street I live in.

From men who wear anger like a wedding ring, punch fists into shed doors and jaws.

From never quite knowing how to say goodbye.
I'm from passing city limits with tears in my eyes.

I'm from the blue and green of a hospital ward.
I am from all that has happened,
And all that will be.

STRETCH MARKS IN WATER

I Stand Still

The sky is endless on the horizon, paint strokes of cream white float against the bright blue, the sun smiles brightly and the birds sings their melodies. I should be happy, but I'm not.

I pull my teal bike that's rusted and the tires are a little bit flat, down the porch stairs, where the wood groans against the weight. I try to be careful , but I underestimated gravity, as the front wheel hits the soft spot behind my knee, hard. I'm tempted to break my bike in half.

I pedal furiously. The sharp pain behind my knee dissipates as I pay attention to the burn in my lungs and the strain in my thighs. *I cannot break things. I cannot break people,* I tell myself.

When the burn reaches my throat, and my stomach heaves, I stop. My muscles relaxes as I glide along the winding path. Through the searing pain, I can also feel the wind. It's only in this moment that I feel free. But the traffic light stands tall and opposing.

My bike screeches to a stop. The pain catches up to me and I wonder why I have to hurt myself to chase that fleeting feeling. Why do I chase things that aren't for me? Why can't I ever be satisfied? The sky is blue, the sun is shining and the birds are singing. The world is happy.

Even through the motion, no matter how hard I pedal, how long I glide through this path I've been on a thousand times, I stand still.

My gaze follows the horizon towards the empty fields. I wonder, if I venture into the vastness and never stop, will I finally see the beauty of what surrounds me? I like to imagine that I have enough courage to go towards the unknown, and pedal until I'm nothing but skin and bones. I'll then lie in the middle of the field, under the constellation, and listen to my last few breaths, saying, *this is it. I am happy.*

But I stand under the towering traffic light, always wondering.

STRETCH MARKS IN WATER

Same Old

Upstairs, the gentle sobbing of my mother, the heaving of her chest because I'm not as healthy as she wants me to be. I take her hand up and make her feel the bumps on my face until she yanks herself away.

She called it disgusting once, but now she just says nothing. She buys me shape-wear, expensive perfumes and three different kinds of acne creams that smell like chemicals and leave my face red but not smooth. I keep taking her hand, palm-up to remind her that they're still there. I pop them and they grow back, like me. So stubborn under all that makeup.

I lure myself into a spandex trap and text Ella, *is this what death feels like?* Alone in my room, I say, *God is this a poem?* It's uncomfortable, it feels like a poem. God never answers, which is what really makes it poetry.

I pull on spanx and think of death and when I'm done thinking of death, I think of God, and when I'm done thinking of God, I fall backwards onto my bed and try to feel small. It isn't hard.

I think of my mother upstairs.

And then God doesn't answer but Ella does.

STRETCH MARKS IN WATER

A Poem Written Into A Voice Memo On The Toll Road

How many eternities have I lived inside this song? The car wheezes when my father tries to push it up a hill past 60. Nothing is going right today. There is a flea coated dog sleeping on the seat beside me. My friend calls to tell me her mum died. The doctor says the test results are in, and while they cannot say for certain that it is this, they also cannot yet say for certain that it is not.

Meanwhile, the traffic less road stretches before me like a fated envelope. The surrounding trees of my childhood flirt with death; their leaves all tinged with brown while palm trees shake their proud heads at the smoke filled air, as helicopters buzz like mosquitoes in the ear of the afternoon.

The empty lot off the freeway exit that once led to my grandma's now holds a retirement home. The house she died in is now the living place of a new family. On the road's shoulder, a powder blue Camry has its jaws open, while the car's owner bends over its mouth, trying to figure out why it has suddenly stopped talking.

Behind them, the river flicks its tongue at the sky, until the two finally collapse into each other. The song playing through the car speakers dances on and on, its skirt flapping in the wind while the guitar shakes hands with the drums, and the singer's voice side steps into a spin, turning faster and faster as the song widens and drops, until it ruptures across the road, building me a home to live in for another eternity.

STRETCH MARKS IN WATER

II

"The Past Beats Inside Me Like A Second Heart."

- John Banville, The Sea.

I own almost nothing from my past. Every photo has been sitting in a green plastic bag at my mother's house. It's yours after I'm dead, my mother says. She's joking, but she's not joking.

I suppose she's holding onto the bag because she's responsible for losing everything else – and I can't bring myself to argue with her about it. In the green bag is the whole ocean, photos from me and my brother's childhood, which exist up until a certain age. And then nothing exists at all.

It's nearly all been lost – to time, to anger, to violence, to illness, to carelessness.

A loss of self, a loss of memory, a loss of childhood.

My Body Is A Sickness Called Anger (i)

After Lisa Marie Basile

There is an Anne Carson quote from Grief Lessons, that says: *why does tragedy exist?*

Because you are full of rage. Why are you full of rage? Because you are full of grief.

When I study my anger, and my mother's anger, and her mother's anger, I see our anger as a processing of grief. It is a grieving of unlived dreams, of plans put off to tend to obligations, of hopeful selves which were replaced by enforced duties, of loves that hardened, of childhood that were painful, of families that did not show us the validation and care we craved.

We are in grief, and so, we are furious.

STRETCH MARKS IN WATER

My Body Is A Sickness Called Anger. (ii)

After Lisa Marie Basile

I want to break my family's cyclical fury. I want to validate myself in a way I have been searching for my whole life – in a hope for apology in my mother, in the safety I create with my friends. I want to forgive myself for the ways I have taken out a hurt too big for me to understand.

Anger is a twisting, mangled root, and working through it involves breaking the soil to trace it to the stem.

In other instances, my mother would make a callous remark, one that I would typically respond to with controlled patience, but – perhaps, because of a bad day or maybe my defenses being worn thin – I could not handle at that moment. I would begin to scream, cry, punch myself in the face, tear at my hair and bang my head against the bedroom walls. The rage would take over, transforming me, like it transformed my grandmother, into a thing made wild by its own hurt.

Each time I succumbed to rage, I would be filled with self loathing. My anger made me feel weak and uncontrollable. Following each break down, i would tell myself, it will be better next time. If I just hold my tongue a lil bit longer. If I just learn to be more quiet, silently hoping to will myself into the shelter of invisibility.

It was not simply that I was spilling out fury senselessly, it was that I didn't know how to exist beneath the weight of memory. A slight tone of rudeness in someone's voice would provoke me into tears. A swell of life – suggestions from my old friends – even if they were rooted in the desire to help would cause my defenses to harden. Criticism from them would feel like a return to helplessness. In all of these instances, I often communicated my feelings unproductively; my voice whittled into a tool for rage, my anger a thick flame beating hot and resolute.

I text Sam, and she says; *Although I know you're very angry with them, and you have valid reasons to be, I think it's still a good call to pick apart the language you've both used and see how you both bring out toxic bits of each other.*

I want expressing my hurt to leave me feeling well-articulated and clear-headed, not ashamed. I want to grant myself permission to move forward. I want to keep writing myself into understanding; my fingers deep in thick soil, my anger an uprooted thing drying out on the dirt, shriveling in the clarifying sunlight.

Untangling Anger

When the anger is a flame beating hot inside your stomach. When it grows into a blaze threatening to consume you as you listen to men in power tell women – who share stories that sound so much like ours – that they are liars, fill a bucket of water and leave it by the flame's side. Turn the music high. Run into a field with your bare naked body and let the reeds rush through you like wind.

There are times to be loud. When the world rustles around you, its buzzes engulfing all slowness you contain, let yourself be taken by its unending noisiness. When the apology text comes in, and he has wrung out his rage – soaked words and shoves sorry like a plate of food through the slit of your door.

When the stove won't turn on, and the gas whines of it, too tired to exhale into flame. When the day stretches into afternoon and you're still in bed, reading a onslaught of headlines naming men who will not be held accountable for their actions. Leave the screen open and join the day.

There is an infinite amount of time to be sad. Your grief will not be contained by today. But today still holds the possibility of continuation. Move forward into it. Anger is a dessert you can walk across all night, searching for repentance. But for now, there is a need for a fire, and dinner to be cooked, and people to be fed.

Sit down. Spread the butter over the bread. The world will be waiting for you when you are ready to join it.

STRETCH MARKS IN WATER

III

Mamia

While staying for months in the normal heights apartment of my cousins', i remained in the same mile radius. Slipped out to the store across the street while they were still asleep - quietly chopped the potatoes and onions, so when they woke up, there would be the smell of a meal to share.

I can sense the capabilities of my grandmother inside of me while my hands work over the food. Returning to when I'd shuck corn with her while the radio cooed in the background. An afternoon of pulling cobwebby coating from the pale yellow kernels, my hands tangled in thin white strings, all for a quick Merci at the end of the meal.

My mother wants to know why her front door remains unlocked, and the pantry filled, and I, at the rustle of a guest, hurry downstairs to ask if they have eaten. When I visited my grandma in Orile Imo, she laid out the bread and butter, the pot of steaming pasta, as i mixed the sauce.

While pushing me away from the soapy basin resting in the sink, she insisted I take a dozen strawberry cupcakes and an assortment of stone fruits on the bus with me.

A few years later, back with my mother, I bound up the familiar stairs first. The door pulled open to reveal the smell of onions on the stove and a distant swoop of the radio. Cloaked in the haziness of aging, my grandmother squinted at me in confusion, for a second, uncertain of who I was, but still asking,

Are you hungry?

Cathedral

My body has not once been a temple.

I remember years ago,

sitting poolside with my grandmother,

her spidery, veined hands touching

my knee;

Your body is a grand temple,

only those who are holy are worth admittance.

And her stern sincerity made me laugh.

My body is a wet, lush jungle.

My body has been trampled

through and lived in.

Destroyed, burned,

yet always continues to rebirth

itself from the rubble and debris.

Am I any less for this?

My body is a mystery,

a slow wafer on the tip of a

school boy's tongue.

A dark, cool place to rest your

weary head.

A place to let your feet press

into the rich soil and feel like

maybe you can call this home.

I think one time,

a man with dark hair and light

eyes thought he could reduce me

to mere trees and rain, not knowing

The jungle is not a safe place.

Unlike those with temples for bodies,

my heart lives deep in a hidden cave

guarded with sharp memories that

feel like claws.

 My memories have teeth, and my heart has a brain.

STRETCH MARKS IN WATER

The Strawberry Patch

There's a poem about forgiveness I have been trying to write, but don't know how to. So instead, I write about the wild strawberry patch in my grandmother's backyard.

How she spent the summer watering them, picking them, making them into jam. How she would hum softly under her breath in French. How her hands would brush over the berries as gently as they outlined the heads of her children.

After her 81st birthday, the home was too much work for her to maintain alone, so her son sold it to a young couple who wanted to visit the country on weekends.

The night she put the keys in the couples' hands, she fell asleep listening to soft French songs without humming along.

By the time she was 82, the strawberry patch was overgrown; untended to, unloved. She swore off strawberries for most of that summer, but one day in July, she took the bus to the store and bought three bushels of them.

That afternoon, she sang *Ne Me Quitte Pas* loudly as she filled the counters with fresh-baked strawberry cake. I found her at night with a slice In hand and a smile on her face.

She offered one to me as she said,

This is how to move on.

This is how you mourn what you loved

and forgive yourself for losing it.

STRETCH MARKS IN WATER

Mothers

After DAUGHTER.

(In a journal written in my mother's writing, for her mother).

Ma, your body got an illness that

was not invisible.

When the disease came, so did

the calls, asking if you were okay.

Finally, you got an illness that made

others believe you deserved to see

a doctor.

Ma, they saw your angry gapes of

skin and shuddered, but i could

only stare at the wreckage.

It did not surprise me to see your

body destroy itself,

I quietly lived with it happening to

your head for twenty three years.

"We think we no longer love our dead, but that is because we do not remember them: suddenly, we catch sight of an old glove and burst into tears."

– Anne Carson.

Bones

Life doesn't stop still for anybody. That's what you'd say with your voice hoarse, barely above a whisper. You held my face between your hands and felt the tremors. Your lips pulled tight across your face, almost touching from ear to ear. I always thought you looked funny like this; a smile of a clown betrayed by sunken eyes.

You would always say, *life doesn't care who it hurts. You get hurt and you go on.*

I heard your voice when the neighborhood kids didn't want me to play with them, because I always wore the same old, red, ratty sweater. I heard your voice when I didn't pass the test, even though I read the same pages a thousand times. I heard your voice when a girl left a mark she could never undo. So I went on.

Those strings words sang songs in my head as I looked at you. I held your hand and I didn't feel you shake anymore. You were still. The permanent line etched onto your face didn't look strained as before. It was almost as if you were smiling - as if to say this time, i couldn't go on.

I didn't hear your voice anymore, not when you went into the black pit of hell until you were nothing but bones. I tried to recall what you'd always say, but i didn't remember.

You see, grandma, as i watched a sapling grow from your remains, I realized i didn't want to live like you. Life hurts who it wants to hurt; i cannot deny that. But you're wrong to just move on. You're wrong to not allow yourself to feel. My tears are endless now: pouring into the palm of my hands. You didn't cry at all grandma, so let me cry for you.

STRETCH MARKS IN WATER

IV

The Depression Gets Real With Me

We

We are breaking you apart to see if

you are strong enough.

No. *Patient enough*

No. *Hopeful enough.*

No.

We are pulling you apart bit by bit,

because it is fun to do so,

because this is just how it works.

There is no satisfying answer.

Nothing you did to deserve this

brain, this fear and us.

But here we are.

All yours and refusing to leave.

We are breaking you open because

your childhood and illness is

somewhere too deep to touch and

it's going to open its hungry jaws to

swallow you with or without us.

This isn't about reason.

This is about seeing how many times

you can choke on hope and still ask

for another spoonful.

This is about taking away everything

you rely on and watching you scramble

to new ways to live.

We are giving you all of this aching

to see what you can do with it.

STRETCH MARKS IN WATER

Bracelets

(I)

I never wondered why we didn't have a sharp knife in the house. Microwave meals require no preparation.

After dinner, in the evenings, my grubby little hands with nails bitten down to the beds would trace the lines of scars on my mother's arms, grazing the textures of thick, black lines with dumb fingertips.

For hours we would carefully thread beads from a massive organizer onto plastic lace, making the bracelets she wore from wrist to elbow, to hide.

(II)

Schoolteacher's words fell on the deaf ears of my present body, my mind off in any fictional world I could find.

As a child, like many others, if I ever got my hands on a thumbtack, I could spend hours sticking it through the top layers of skin. On the tips of my fingers, marveling blandly at the lack of pain, addicted to and unexcited by the small victory over my body.

It is with this same bemusement that, years later,

I would break open razors in bathrooms with locked doors, to access their coveted essence; blades.

(III)

The thing about hitting rock bottom is that sometimes it does get even worse. No amount of suffering protects you from any more.

My hands shook more threading beads onto bracelets than they ever did, calmly and meticulously tracing heredity in thin, straight lines from the base of my palm. My first unsuccess was a knife in the bathroom of the retailing shop my mother managed. She told me; *if you want to do it right, go vertically. Parallel.*

When I ended up in the hospital for a stomach ulcer and an enlarged spleen, the triage nurse grilled me about the neatly-filed scars and their origins until I had the courage to drop my gaze and say; *that's not why I'm here.* The doctors in the psych ward of emergency never frowned at me as deeply as she did then. Once you've seen it all –

(IV)

I only ever ran away twice. The time I left for the longest, I spent most of my rebellion in an unfinished building next to my house. I scraped my thigh climbing up the rusted metal ladder.

My body is covered in similar stories of injury. Born pigeon-toed and graceless, such was my norm; scraped, skinned, bruised, sliced.

By some definition, it's all self-harm. A momentary lapse in the instinct for self-preservation. My wrist tells its own story; that of someone who needed release. All the layering of tracks amounts one story alone. And it's not even my best one.

Emotional Abuse Works Like This

You're screamed at, and then not knowing any better, you stand up for yourself. You think this is a way of being strong, you think this is a defense tactic, but this only provokes more screaming. Going silent provokes more screaming too, but usually keeps it the threat to the minimum. It keeps it just at screaming and not a shove down the stairs, or an order to pack your things and leave.

So you learn how to go silent. How to play dead. How to cry silently. How to swallow noise. How to wipe your cheeks, get out of the car and go about your day.

You learn.

And when the screaming has stopped, when you are at home with them or out to dinner and there're all smiles, all asking for favors, all questions. You're still hurt and annoyed and want to ask them, *how? How can you speak to me like that? How can you pretend you did not say those words? How can you have forgotten?*

But you've learned. So you listen to, *can you lend me some money? Can you take out the trash? How was your day?* And you play dead. You swallow the noise. And sometimes, it doesn't matter who is speaking to you, it doesn't matter if they're a friend, it doesn't matter if their criticism is constructive, it doesn't matter.

You've learned.

Any sort of speaking, any raising of the voice, any insult and you play dead.

STRETCH MARKS IN WATER

Pattern Of Abuse

Our thirty seconds of small talks are a half-inflated balloon floating calmly towards the ceiling. One flick of my tongue and I could pop it. But I keep my carefully sharpened teeth good and nice in my mouth.

My mother's voice is desperate in my head, insisting, *no one likes a commotion.* In the next room, I spot my friends dancing - happy, carefree, grateful to be out.

I imagine smashing a glass into the wall while looking straight at him. I imagine screaming in his face and demanding he leave. The music stopping, the laughter filtering out, the fear spreading across my friends' faces.

I want to ruin his night, but instead I smile. A minute later, he is in another conversation, cracking open his fifth drink. The snap of the pull tab reverberating like a giggle. It jolts into my body until I can't distinguish what of me is skin and what is noise. The entire room is buzzing.

I feel his laughter everywhere. A girl touches a tank topped man's arm and winks. Every hand trying to slip up a thigh in the room is glowing red. I blink. The air is flat and too hot. My politeness is a sigh creeping teasingly down my neck.

Suddenly, someone's fingers knock on my shoulder, asking if I am in the line for the bathroom. Above me are a thousand limp balloons popping in succession.

I take a slow sip of my drink. No, I'm sorry, I say, quietly moving out of the way.

This Is How It Goes No Matter Which City I'm In

When my sister asks me how I'm doing and i say, I still have to adjust, what I mean is,

it's been hard.

What I mean is, whenever i think I know loneliness, it comes to me with a softer voice.

What I mean is, it is a lot easier to stay in bed when there are fewer people asking where

i've been.

And every time I want to call a friend, to ask for help, I remember that everyone has their own wounds to tend to. What I mean is, I know how worry can eat up a day.

When she asks me if I'm happy here and I say, I like it here, sure. What I mean is,

I'm becoming a surer version of myself but I don't know how many times I will sob in the back of a taxi before this growing is over.

What I mean is I'm writing poems about suicide in a place with more rocks and trees.

V

My Friend Once Threw Up On My Front Porch

Drunk, my door a haven she knew

would always let her in, she spent

so many nights as the other half of

my twin bed.

I've written so many love poems that

I forgot my first love was sisterhood.

That I forgot the two weeks I didn't

sleep to give her medicine after surgery,

Forgot palms outstretched like

roadmaps, reminding me

there's always a way home.

STRETCH MARKS IN WATER

We can not ask those we love to remain versions of themselves that we know, just because this gives us comfort. We must see outside of what serves us, and honour/trust their growth, even if it is in a direction separate from us. We must sift through our fears of losing them, while allowing them to become themselves.

If we leave space for them, if we respect them, it is more likely they will come back - that they will feel safe and seen with us. We can't expect they'll return, or demand them to - but clinging will not contain them. It is dishonorable to them because we are asking them to restrict their growth, to us because we are denying ourselves the experience of working through our feelings.

Heat Wave

On the patio of the bamboo groove,

I'm crying while reading poems about

the death of a brother.

The inevitability of loss courses through

them like a song - no one around me can

hear it. They are busy clearing their throats,

spooning fruits into their mouths, checking

something or the other on their phones.

It is 80 degrees in October and the sweat clings to my back as I run down 25th street.

I'm alone again; just the other night, the friend I have loved for the last year told me she did not know who she was.

And when I asked her, *do you want to stay with me?* Silence spread through my bedroom as the thin stream of the alley light filtered in and we laid there, her, pushed against the pillows, still wearing her jeans, ready to leave soon. And me, buried under three quilts, fiddling with the torn hem of one of them.

Before she left, I pulled her in for a hug, pressed my nose to the soft of her neck and she did the same. Her nose against my neck and her head on my shoulder, as I ran my hands through her hair and thanked her for everything in the last

year.

Please, don't start drinking or refuse

to talk to anyone about this, I said.

And she nodded.

Now I think of all the quiet moment

she will have in her bedroom,

the green cups pilling up on her desk.

The garlic frying on the stove and the

coffee waiting to be pressed down,

The ways she will go on living without

me there to see it.

Daniella George – My Friend From Down Under

I tried to find the right metaphor for

the storm but I ended up mumbling your

name.

I can hear your bones break like thunder.

I can hear your cries against my

windowpane, thousands of miles from

where you are.

You never thought I would stop

running but I did.

I still remember the day you begged

my heart to settle down.

I remember our little dance in the

terrace, two young people in the night,

experiencing forever in twelve hours.

You are the reason why I feel sad

over the sound of singing cicadas

and heartbeats.

You are the reason why I stopped

leaving things unfinished.

Last night, your sister called to tell

me how you're doing.

I wonder if your scars still hurt when

it's six degrees outside.

I want to cover your shoulders with

words and moonlight, until it softens,

until you stop putting your hand on

your chest at 2AM, to keep it from

howling.

I don't remember what type of storm

you are anymore,

But I still remember you when it rains.

Bless The Crazy Femmes.

For how much they endure silently.

For the survival game they play against

their heads everyday.

For the hurt in them that wants to

swallow the softness.

May they know comfort in their bodies

May their heads not win and the world

be theirs.

Bless The Healing

Bless what is hurting.

Bless the healing.

Bless this body, soft with wanting.

Bless the names of the lost which we carry.

Bless unveiling possibility in fear.

Bless my sleeping craziness, may it

slumber till I die.

Bless the things that grew in-place of

what was taken.

Bless what tried to kill us and now must

watch us survive.

NOTES

The first part of the book's epigraph is from Ocean Vuongs "On Earth We're Briefly Gorgeous."

The title "The Past Beats Inside Me Like A Second Heart" is from John Banville's "The Sea." (Novel)

"My Body Is A Sickness Called Anger" (I & II) Is After Lisa Marie Basile. An essay from the book "Burn It Down", edited by Lilly Dancyger.

"My Body Is A Sickness Called Anger" (I) borrows a quote from Anne Carson's book, "Grief Lessons."

"Mothers" is after a musical band called DAUGHTER. It is the title of a song on the album "Not To Disappear."

"Bones" borrows a phrase from Anne Carson's poem "Wildly Constant."

STRETCH MARKS IN WATER

ACKNOWLEDGEMENTS

I would like to thank a few people in no particular order, for helping this book come to life.

Ogundele Sheriff, for all the help you rendered in the process of bringing this book to life. For reading this book in manuscript form and giving me reasons why this work matters.

Remi Akinwande - Jordan, for every moment of your active belief in my work, for inspiring me with yours.

Banji Coker, for always seeing me and rooting for me, you believed in this book so much that I did too. Thank you a thousand times over for being there.

Bailey, for your words of kindness and support when i thought i couldn't do it.

Daniella and Sam. Thank you, Ella, for being my darling friend. Sam, for the many years of loving friendship.

And always – my mother, Oluwakorede, for telling me stories of your past and present self. You made me and my work possible in this world. Thank you for all these years of fierce and unwavering love.

To YOU, the reader, thank you for taking the time to understand, grieve, learn, love and grow with me. All the love.

About The Author

Odule . O'Sussane strives to explore the enormity of our cosmos with the linguistic filigree that is poetry. She considers herself an apprentice when it comes to wordsmithing, but appreciates your appreciation.

STRETCH MARKS IN WATER

Made in the USA
Columbia, SC
15 September 2020